Questions in Jamaican Patois

poems by

Yasmin Morais

Finishing Line Press
Georgetown, Kentucky

Questions in Jamaican Patois

ACKNOWLEDGMENTS

The Uncivil War: *Previously published in The Potomac, 2013*

Half The Sky: *Previously published on Pen and Prosper Blog*

The Road to Respect: *Originally published in Nursing Science Quarterly*

Publisher: Leah Huete de Maines
Editor: Christen Kincaid
Cover Art: Danielle Boodoo-Fortune
Author Photo: Mikayla Lindsay
Cover Design: Elizabeth Maines McCleavy

Order online: www.finishinglinepress.com
also available on amazon.com

Author inquiries and mail orders:
Finishing Line Press
PO Box 1626
Georgetown, Kentucky 40324
USA

Contents

To my Carey, Dobson, Jacobs, Lindsay, Madden, and Morais tribes
You inspire me every day. Keep on questioning.

Yahtzee

On nights when winds howl and hiss
She curls, c-shaped at my feet
Her brindle coat a warm comforter.
I hear her gentle snore
As she drifts off to dream fitful dog dreams.
This rescue in a way rescued me.
The younger daughter's nagging for a dog won out
And Yahtzee arrived before my right breast mastectomy.
In her own way, she helped me make sense
Of cancer (if one ever can).

We bond now more than ever; me easing into empty nest phase.
My kids who begged incessantly for her
Are now grown and gone to stroll through halls in college towns.
Now, we take unhurried evening walks
She, leading the way with boundless curiosity
Sniffing at every blade of grass.
I find myself talking to her more these days—you
Tend to do that in an empty, quiet house.
And Yahtzee looks up at me with quizzical eyes,
Perhaps grateful for my undivided attention.

Cold Ground

"Cold ground was my bed last night, and rock was my pillow too"
Talkin' Blues. Bob Marley and the Wailers.
Cold ground.
Frozen thoughts stopped in their tracks.
Icy stares and icicle daggers drawn
In a cold, cold war.
Hibernating dreams on hold
Buried in deep leaf burrows.
Temperature not lowered on unbridled anger
Winds of adversity unrelentingly blowing
On this stone-cold land.
In this sub-zero space, life is still there.
And metamorphosis and promise.
While hope incubates
Slowly, we edge closer to our promised spring.

Camera

Ubiquitous camera—ever staring,
always following; body-shaming me and you.
Right on cue, we pose, we smile,
even through our deepest pain.
Perilously, we hang by cliff sides,
craving Instagram likes for that perfect selfie,
not grasping the lesson that some things
just need to be watched in awe.
Camera—intruder of my cluttered headspace
capturing a thousand emotions on my bewildered face.
Body cameras—capturing knees on necks,
heartless blows and inhumanity.
Judges, *in camera*
making and breaking laws
that circumscribe you and me.

The Uncivil War

Funny, it wasn't classified a war.
despite the final death toll,
and a nation turned on itself.
I dodge gunshots
trying to start my evening commute.
Remaining mute
about my political allegiance.
Speaking would be suicidal.

"Don't wear a red shirt, for God's sake,"
my mother scolded my brother.
Red, not just the color of blood,
but Manley red,
socialism red,
PNP red.
Our very apparel came under siege.
So, my poor brother could not wear
his green shirt either,
fearing being linked to
Seaga green,
capitalism green,
JLP green.

Just who were the trigger pullers?
It was so easy then to name, and blame, and shame.
But so hard to tell in an uncivil war
where politics, corruption, and drugs morphed,
and Uncle Sam, Cuba, JLP and PNP
made strange bedfellows in 1970s Jamaica.

Nine Point Eight One

9.81
He made easy strides,
effortless glides
into the history books.

9.81 seconds
of pure thrill
down the track
shouts of "Usain, Usain"
at his back.

At the finish line
he looked left
he looked right
dazzling smile
leaving the competition
stunned and speechless!

Our Bolt, ever playful, ever gracious
One beautiful final Olympic gift
to this little island rock,
to the world.

Our Bolt
Large
Phenomenal
Jamaican
Legend.

Heart Space
     (For Dobby)

My memories of you are kept in that deep heart space
protected and watered every now and then
by sad or joyous tears. When Alzheimer's took your memory and words,
I reminded you of big brother jokes out of the long ago, especially
the Edgewater one when you chased away a prospective suitor
who had interrupted my homework.

When miles stood between us, your humor
made the distance easier to bear.
With grace, you tolerated my song requests.
When life storms did their destructive worse,
you soldiered on bravely. I watched you battle Covid.
Fortis Cadere Cedere Non Potest!
Though you fell, you never yielded really.

That evening, your soul soared to new realms
to sit near peaceful streams and hear wonderful sounds
to sing new songs with Ma Belle, Mama, and the rest of your choir
to interrogate angels and saints
to have sweet, sweet dreams
and rest at last in the arms of your Savior.

New Air
(For George Floyd)

I feel rage and my heart aches
for the ache inflicted on you.
The shameless cruelty of it all.
George, I wish I could have soothed
your brow and wiped your tears
in your last eight minutes
of fear and torment, or held your hand as you gasped
and begged for air.I wish I could have kicked away
that iron knee, weaponized by
a power-hungry, hate-filled soul.

You are at peace now, safe in
your mama's loving arms.
Your skin, no longer an offense.
You walk in power in a new land,
singing your freedom songs,
your redemption songs.
George, you breathe new, pure air now.
Your soul soars above the filth, decay, and dross;
above the evil philosophy that holds one race
superior, and another inferior.
You are chanting down the Babylon system
with Marley, Garvey, Malcolm, and King.
Sing your new songs, George. Sing.

Questions in Jamaican Patois

Wha you fi do when you back gainst di wall,
and yu want fi bawl, but di tears won't come at all?
Wha you fi do when you heart bruk in two
and di smaddy you really check for just don't love you?

Wha you fi seh when you feel like you cyan go on
and you just want fi run?
Whey you fi go when you feel boxed in?
When di rain a fall and the dutty still tough?

When people a gi you a 6 for a 9
and others just nuh want fi tow di line?
Is every little ting really going to be alright?
Will you really see clearly when the rain is gone,
and your many rivers have been crossed?

Half The Sky

They say we hold up half the sky,
yet every day daughters sigh
and mothers cry.

Misogynistic rants tear us down.
Boundaries are set:
"You can't do that yet!"

Hold your head up,
square those shoulders.
Let your smile shine through.
Be your own you.
Don't apologize,
just strategize.

This is your day;
this is your time.
Princess, you can cross that finish line!

Postcard from Havana

At Havana airport, separated by a curtain of glass,
we air-touched. Our interminable gaze kept at bay the many
questions
crying out for answers that perhaps our hearts did not want to know.
Ridiculous—me leaving and you arriving
because you refused to be bound by time and order.
Our together trip, fragmented. So, I'd sojourned Havana solo.

I smiled a week later at the postcard you sent,
and what you said was your most expensive phone call ever.
Memories are the only roads and stories the only bridges
to haunting flashes.
A postcard and my sweet nostalgia are permanent keepsakes
of a love that could have been.

The Day of Small Things

Prepping and preening for that
perfect selfie; everything on fleek
while inside, our better sides yearn to break free
and shine through our rough and tumble days.
Mean, cold stares and glares
 cause our lips to freeze,
half-opened for that ready smile.
Our 'hi' and 'how are you?" are stillborn
as hurried, frazzled souls try to keep pace
on the treadmill of life.
You see but don't see me.
We all steal glances at fellow travelers
on crowded commutes, while raised books
meet our gaze, and heads are bowed low
in a never-ending obeisance to our electronic gods.
But, once in a while, kindred spirits
cross our paths.
We slow our steps and find and follow
 meandering and timeless roads to peace.
Our better selves unite.
No competition, just pure agape love.
Then knitted hearts and minds
give thanks for the day of small things.

Accents

"Could you please speak a little louder?"
"I can't hear a word you are saying."
Accents:
Oftentimes equated with stupidity.
No time to listen keenly.
No wisdom found in lilting, foreign tongues.

It seems so hard to take the time to bridge the divide,
to find commonality, explore our shared humanity.
"What did you say? I don't understand you."
"Is English your first language?"
"Yes, we were ruled by the British."
"I don't know any other language."
Accents.

Black River Nostalgia

The gentle Black River meanders through
Grandma's town and feeds St. Bess,
The breadbasket of Jamaica.
St. Bess—where street vendors tempt with
peppered shrimps, and pineapples so
sweet, they scratch your throat.

Black River, where mama tried and failed
to earn her Girl Guide badge in swimming.
Years later, on my first visit,
I saw the little schoolhouse where,
with a six-year-old's rage at a flogging,
my mother had bitten her teacher's leg.

Belle's Property

She cleaned offices by night,
always holding on tight
to the dream of owning
a piece of the rock.

Every pound and shilling mattered.
Soon, she withdrew from the Bank of Mattress,
enough to pay down on a small property in Kingston.
She stared at the receipt with incredulity.
Semi-literate single mother
on her way to owning land?

One more baby and many hardships later,
Belle lost her property and her dreams.
My grandma went to her grave
feeling smart-talking lawyers deliberately cheated her.

Belle of Black River

It was the cow foot and beans.
Grandma Belle, who could not stand the taste,
had devoured half a pot,
driven by a craving she could not understand.

Frantic mom shuttled her to the village midwife,
ostensibly to check on the old lady.
The midwife with trained eyes,
spun the clueless Belle around.
"Tell your mother all is well".

"All is well", the cheery Belle announced on reaching home.
A stinging slap caught Belle's bewildered face.
All was not well!
Belle learned that day
of the new life growing inside her.

Rain

Rain, our collective tears
washing from a pain-filled earth
anger, bigotry and
a thousand years of hurt.

Rain, our cleansing.
removing innocent
and not so innocent blood
spilled on our streets of rage.

Rain, our comfort.
a lullaby for insomniacs,
pent up and tense
who by each raindrop
edge closer to that needed sleep.

Weekend in Silent Hill, Manchester

Silent Hill.
Truly silent, except for evening crickets.
The fog-covered mountains
and a Christiana-fed cold called for
sweaters and socks.

Full-moon nights.
Silent fluttering fireflies.
Cold river water. Crocodiles?
Wading, nonetheless.

All this, while navigating too Zacca's growing
 Infatuation and his silent admiration
that my sixteen-year-old heart did not understand.

My Mother and The Other Woman

They turned up at the church outing
at *Puerto Seco* beach.
My mother and the other woman,
both wearing dresses made from the same fabric.

My mother, the eternal fashionista,
was livid and humiliated.
Miss Doris, the other woman,
uncomfortable and embarrassed,
tried to be nice to my sister and me.

It did not help matters any that the hit song of the day,
"I would like you and my sweetheart to be friends"
sounded loud and mocking
from the beach party in full progress.

The Way of the Butterflies

I wonder often where butterflies go
after flitting over my head.
Light and delicate wings
softly propel them
upward, onward, heavenward.
Defying boundaries
Brightening skies.

Such freedom!
Unrestrained and schedule-less,
monarchs, viceroys, and black swallowtails
pass farmlands and lakes,
clouds and rainbows,
while earth-bound mortals watch in awe.

Billy

Beneath the radar of stern-faced nuns,
my friends passed me love notes
from a boy named Billy.
He'd slipped them through the Berlin-wall-like
chain-link fence separating St. Aloysius Boys' and St. Joseph's Girls'
Schools.
My pre-teen heart was ignorant of his existence and crush.

Dada, open to hearing such girl stuff,
laughed at the notes I shared.
Love songs somehow have perfect timing in my life:
"Which way you're going, Billy" was the hit of the day,
and the boy named Billy went off to high school,
fading out of my life.

Bottom Line

Bottom line?
Red blood coursing through our veins,
never mind hues of white, brown, chocolate, black.

Despite attempts at differentiation, our hearts feel pain,
get broken and burn with anger and frustration.
Salty tears fall from blue, green, and brown eyes,
weary from grief and injustice.

And when death makes its claim, we descend
to cold mother earth, where race, class, ethnicity
and social importance lose all their significance.

The Road to Respect

I spoke.
You listened.
I felt valued and honored.
You shared your opinion.
I trusted your wisdom.

The circle of respect was complete.
We saw in each other's eyes our common humanity.
Now, moving to a zone of mutual affirmation,
we felt safe to trust, and learn, and nurture
in the give-and-take of life.

Cocktail Parties

Dutifully you attend.
Periodically, of course, superiors
make mental headcounts.
Networking is the mantra.
Upward mobility is at stake.

So, you sip your wine.
pretending to listen,
the way you do at times
when your six-year-old
recounts an action-packed day.

"It is so hard being a pilot's wife".
"We bought a new yatch last week".
Inflated egos' pretensions
float over your head like a cloud.
And you would give anything
to trade this scene for one
with your animated and sincere six-year old.

Snowstorms

Billions of frenetic snowflakes,
softly drifting to the waiting earth.
Hardened icicles
like daggers drawn,
perched on eaves,
awaiting unsuspecting victims.

Snowstorms of life,
unrelenting, denying thaw
leaving cold hearts
and frozen minds
on the icy, slippery highway of life.

Toronto Time

Toronto time.
Caribana dancing.
Dancing also around office politics
and the cultural clashes
of an unfulfilled immigrant.

Learning to be politically correct.
Toronto time. Self-imposed exile.
Truly a border woman
on days when I felt stateless.

Toronto time. Yet also fun times
of basking in the Lake Ontario breeze.
Drinking with the Diaspora.
Finding love, finding me.
Toronto time.

Poetically Correct

Once in a while,
poets may feel compelled
to verbally wander through
the labyrinths of power,
calling out policies that place yokes
of hardship on already dissed and
dis-empowered constituents.

Mighty poetic pens
must sometimes take a stab at
those polititricksters
who have long forgotten
the casters of the votes
that enthroned them
on their seats of power

The Green Bay Massacre

They were promised jobs.
Seven hopeful men
jumped at the chance
to find dignity through work.

Weird times.
Political warfare.
Battle lines drawn.
Democracy hung by a fragile thread.
Soldiers transported them
to the rolling Hellshire hills.
Green Bay was peaceful in the night.

The shimmering lights of Kingston looked like diamonds.
In an instant, a savage brutality took hold.
Five men lay crumpled and lifeless,
the powerless on the political totem pole.
Senseless executions.
Crawling through the cane fields,
quivering in fear,
two men escaped to tell a nation's shame.

Learning Math

"Girl in the blue clip, go to the chalkboard and solve number one!"
I'm numb, feeling so dumb.
Nameless girl in a blue clip, in a Kingston Technical classroom.
Yet I manage to walk with square shoulders,
head erect to face certain humiliation.

My palms glisten with sweat. The chalk slips.
Figures dance within my head, while theorems escape me.
Sine and cosine are playing games in my mind.
Quadratic equation. What a situation!

He shifts from the window and heads towards me,
his white shoes dazzling
in the Monday morning sun.
"You idiot, sit! Class, follow while I solve."
And I try to be invisible and wait for the merciful bell.

Jamaica Day-Dreaming

Ackee and codfish.
Golden fried dumplings.
Festival!
Ripe plantains and hot cocoa
awaken memories
of a Negril beach.
Seven miles of glorious golden sand.

I dream of Holywell and the Blue Mountains,
colorful hummingbirds and myriad butterflies.
But the dazzling snow on my balcony
brings me back to reality.
My Jamaica daydream ends
And I slowly savor the last morsel
of my Sunday morning breakfast

Silence

Silence.
Deafening.
Defining moments.
Clarifying unshared thoughts.
Creating space for introspection.
Opportunity for mental renewal.

Silence.

All these, and yet so wounding
for the one who needs to hear
words of reconciliation.

Silence.
A cloud of uncertainty.
Perhaps finality.
A closure of what might have been.
Silence.

The Night Season

Our night seasons come and sometimes last long
but in them we know whether we're really strong.
Friends leave, love's lost,
dreams die so fast.
For comfort or rules for living
there's no one to ask.

In the night season, you're often alone.
No one's beside you, you have to make it on your own.
But a part of you you've never met, comes to the fore,
giving you new strength to face life once more.

In the night season, there's chance for new growth.
Old props are thrown out, doubt gives way to hope.
Love is renewed and patience revived.
In the night season, your hopes never died.

Yasmin Morais was born in Jamaica. She attended the University of the West Indies (Mona) where she completed her Bachelor of Arts (Spanish) and Master of Science (Government, with an International Relations focus). She later moved to Toronto, Canada, where she completed a Master of Science in Information Studies at the University of Toronto. Yasmin also holds a Bachelor of Laws (LLB, Honors) from the University of London.

She currently works as a law librarian and has published articles in academic journals such as the *International Journal of Legal Education,* and *Legal Reference Services Quarterly.* Her research guides on Scottish Legal History and Cuban Law have also been published in *Globalex.* In addition, she published a book review on the international law blog, *DipLawMatic Dialogues.* Yasmin has also written a book chapter on her law library residency at the Georgetown Law Library, which was published by Libraries Unlimited in 2011. She has also published two reports for the project, *Monitoring the Legal Response to Covid 19 in Latin America* and the *Caribbean.19: https://lawlibrariansmonitoringcovid19.wordpress.com/2020/05/04/ caricom-oecs/*

Her book, *Legal Research Methods for the English-speaking Caribbean,* which she co-authored with fellow law librarian, Yemisi Dina, was published in March 2024 by Carolina Academic Press.

Yasmin's poems were published in *The Potomac, Nursing Science Quarterly,* and *Pen and Prosper.* To promote the work of Caribbean poets, Yasmin created the blog Poets of the Caribbean: *poetsofthecaribbean.blogspot.com.* She has reviewed Pamela Mordecai's Subversive Sonnets *http://poetsofthecaribbean.blogspot. com/2012/09/subversive-sonnets-review.htmlh* and has also been a guest blogger on *Pen and Prosper, Writing a Novel in Thirty Days: https://penandprosper.blogspot.com/2012/11/guest-post-by-poet-and-writer-yasmin.html?m=0.*

Her short story, *Rashida's Letter*, placed third in the Tallahassee Writer's Association competition and was later published in the *Seven Hills Review*. See link: *https://www.amazon.com/Seven-Review-Tallahassee-Writers-Association/dp/1481148818* Yasmin was also a winner of the Gotham Writers Very Short Story Competition: *https://www.writingclasses.com/contest/very-short-story-contest-2014.*

In her spare time, she loves to travel, play badminton, and run.

www.ingramcontent.com/pod-product-compliance
Lightning Source LLC
Chambersburg PA
CBHW020221090426
42734CB00008B/1162